Preparing for Spring

For Maggie FitzGerald Regan

3/6/2012
Dear Esther –
thank you
for such
attentic !
warmest
wishes,

Nell Regan   Nell.

Preparing for Spring

ARLEN
HOUSE

Published in 2007 by
ARLEN HOUSE
an imprint of Arlen Publications Ltd
PO Box 222
Galway
Phone/Fax: 353–86–8207617
Email: arlenhouse@gmail.com

Distributed in North America by
SYRACUSE UNIVERSITY PRESS
621 Skytop Road, Suite 110
Syracuse, NY 13244–5290
Phone: 315–443–5534/Fax: 315–443–5545
Email: supress@syr.edu

ISBN: 978–1–903631– 61–4, paperback
(a signed and numbered limited edition is also available)

Typesetting ¦ Arlen House
Printing ¦ Betaprint
Cover Image ¦ Sarah FitzGerald
'Abandoned Pomegranates' (2005)
reproduced by courtesy of the artist

Contents

ACKNOWLEDGMENTS

Acknowledgments and thanks are due to the editors of the following journals where some of these poems first appeared: *Poetry Ireland Review, The SHOp, Fortnight, Force 10, Cyphers, Books Ireland, The Stinging Fly* and *The New Writer*. A selection was also previously published in *Breaking the Skin: 21st Century Irish Writing* (Black Mountain Press, 2002) and *Underworld* (Lapwing, 2004).

I would also like to thank Paula Meehan, Eiléan Ní Chuilleanáin, Beth Lewis, Sarah Dobbs, Paula Shields, Jonathan Williams and, very especially, Cathal Ó Searcaigh.

PART I

WATER TO WATER, SALT TO SALT
i.m. Nancy FitzGerald, 1916–2003

I want to tell you about the child;
how she followed a gull with her eyes
then her neck extended, body lifted
and arms outflung so she all but
took flight, with hardly a breath
between seeing and becoming.

I want to tell you about the harbour;
how its wall is an arm I swim within
as salt and sun work an alchemy
in my body; how its cupped hand
is the bell tower of the church whose
stones are sunk below the water,

and I want to tell you about the church;
how its back wall is a great baroque
confection, illuminating the gloom.
But these salted prayers dissolve the tiles
as the sea rises and its undertow hauls
me back to where your coffin set sail.

LIGHT
for Caroline FitzGerald

Light seeps through the curtains, blue-grey,
and over the thrum of my own thoughts
the high pitch of the dawn chorus,

sweet and insistent, reaches my ears.
I rise and pull clothes on,
I've given up on more sleep tonight.

It hardly gets dark in this place;
last night I pulled the curtains on an evening
that dawdled, reluctant to give way.

As I take my tea into the weakly-lit yard
(not night, yet not day) I think of you
in Adelaide Street, a veteran of these early mornings.

The new moon hangs over the broad back of Muckish
and it's less lonely to think that you may be up too;
padding blearily to the kitchen to put the kettle on

and half-listen to the radio; preparing for these
long days of sun that are washing winter away.

GLIMPSES

o

The land takes in

great
breathy gulps of rain

and sighs.

o

There are times
the bog at Cluain Barra

becomes acres of fox,
poised to run.

o

Gorse is on the wane,
its fierce yellows curl
to brown

and so will the days
usher in clematis
and
snowy falls of hawthorn

their growth gathers
pace.

AFTER THE FUNERAL
i.m. Jimmy Simmons 1933–2001

After the funeral, night enters with a brief nod
then takes her leave again. I cannot sleep –

loose earth on your coffin still skitters in my head
and my feet walk me over the bog

a flat path winds through the emptiness
I could be the only one awake on earth.

Meadow sweet dust the air, vetch curl and trail,
wild iris stand tall in marshy pools and buttercups
splay.

Hedges emerge and in the elderflower
a million white blooms confer.

On this wide expanse there is no grief; here
there is all grief and its only gesture is wildflower.

LEENAN FORT, LOUGH SWILLY

is the gorge
colonised
by a flame of montbretia;

the gape
of a chimney breast
where swifts hover;

the mess
stripped of its
hide of imperial brick;

the pivot
of a gun
scourged in granite

whose range
is a mile to sea
where a beam of light

opens out the horizon.

STILLS
Glendalough

Snow is falling,
etching the landscape
to a heightened version of itself.

St. Kevin,
in the tiny hermitage,
stretches his muscles and prepares for spring.

In the dark centre of the lake
there is a stillness
where even the wind declines to blow.

THAT JULY

That July was all portent of autumn.
Even on warm days the sky hung low.
It spat and spilt on the darkened town
and the speckle of tail-lights blurred
red as breath condensed on the windows
of the bus, where I traced words and shapes
with my finger, watched beads of sweat
dribble and gather at the strip of black rubber
by my elbow.
                Staring out of this muggy
universe of steaming hair and damp clothes,
I think I am back at school: I smell new copies
and the bus becomes an open page.

DISPATCHES

i

JCBs swagger up and down
and above the rhythms of the masts,
the clatter and clink of the halyards,
is the loud retort of the pile driver;

they are building between the piers –
a new marina whose struts
envelop the inner harbour
where sun ignites the water in a bitter

February wind. *An easterly like this*
would've had 'em straining,
a fisherman nods to small trawlers,
quiescent at their moorings.

Outside the ice house, as three women
fillet and slice the day's catch,
an old bull seal sits up in the sea,
steadies himself for stinking offcuts.

I sling a mackerel carcass in but,
as he dives, a cormorant cleaves through
the water, flensing off a gobbet of fish,
emerging in triumph. The old bull surfaces,

steadies himself again. A tremor
from the site reverberates
through us and the fisherman looks up
they'll be after this place next.

I am back in this town where I grew up,
where the looped railings of the seafront
are so familiar to my hands that now, walking past,
they reach for its blue, rusted chain to swing

and release so it hits the tree with a woody
thunk and fits snugly into the wound
by which I know each trunk,
its weight made visible in wide lips of bark.

Then on, past a black iron stump
with its orbit of tiles, the ghost of a Victorian
fountain; the day after the explosion
a boy brought a gouge of twisted metal

to show the class, but the teacher
was not impressed. And on,
by the station and the Georgian terrace
where screens flicker in a cream office,

so at odds with the damp flat
it must recall being. I broke into
its derelict basement once
and among the rubble and the dank

found a flattened skeleton, perfect
from its cat skull to tail to splayed legs,
as though whatever force crushed the breath
and flesh from it was still pressing down.

The sea is busy, with light and glitter
and wave. This place was all about
clambering, jumping surefooted from
one sharp edge of granite to the next,

clearing the space between one ridged
wall and another, then belting down
wide slate stairs as salty air
dispersed the tension of home.

With the scent of unpacking
still in the flat, I found my place
to drift; between the tar roof
of the kitchen and the hospital wall.

Charlemont Terrace. Still redolent
of the dark, that winter the power
was off. One night I pleaded to be let
go to bed at five, but the look on my

mother's face sears through my mind.
I did not ask again and sometimes,
still, when I think I have cleared
the sharp edges between a then and

a now, I walk past Charlemont;
my nine-year-old eyes stare, reproachfully,
at the self who walks by the tar roof
of the kitchen and the hospital wall.

EACH HOUSE

I will go back and fill each house
with words; on the blank walls
of departure inscribe the shadow
of an opening door; listen in the cupboard
of each remembered street
for the footsteps of belonging.
Memory will distend itself
from a tea chest smell of dust
and foil and thin paper;
un-crouch from the space created
by a mug nudging a cereal bowl
and the O of a plate meeting
the right angle of the chest.
I will emerge from the pages
of each book lived, to imagine a new reality.

LONG WEEKEND

We move toward the sea in a raw glitter of cars;
leave the city to its pavements mouthing dust.
Received by the scent of sand, marram grass and tar
we set up a brief tenancy on the strand. *Augusts*

we spent here, hesitates my ma and I can nearly see
cigarette smoke snaking toward the dunes, smell
the quinine of her G&T, her low laughter; she
is everywhere, my grandmother and the rituals

that died with her last month. The waves form
and fall along the beach and we are both silent,
both daughter. Later, something urgent
in me stirs and the plangent call of the foghorn

challenges me to love again, much as the sea itself
draws breath and insists the wave be remade.

PART II

UNDERWORLD

I spit dark soil out of my mouth
and try to punch my fists
through the low deep roof of this place.
Mother can you not hear me?
I am here and they have stolen
my words, speak each day in some parody
of my halting stunted talk;
the dark soil blocks my windpipe
I wake at night unable to breathe,
my thighs are leaden and I
am about to sink into a despair,
from which I may never return.

O mother, the wedding was a grim
affair, my hair lank and flesh bulky,
and all I could offer as resistance
was a sullen acceptance
of his body on mine.
I believed that you sat with the gods
but you did not even arm me
for this underground world.

SALMON FISHING

We stand in twos and threes, watch the dark sea pulse
through the narrow mouth of the bay; wait
for the under-belly of a wave to erupt as fish.
Cloud shrouds the mountains – the tip of Errigal
goes under and it spills over and down the back
of Muckish. I watch my feet sink slowly
in the sand as the horizon foams and falls by Tory.
A shout goes up! Three men race across the dunes,
drag the slender anchor onto the boat and clamber in,
one pulling at oars as the others feed the net
in a wide arc back to shore where, hand over hand,
we haul it in, heavy with its catch of water
and two mullet that flicker and slap
in the mesh. A fisherman stamps, with the scrunch
of boot on fish on wet sand the urgent muscle stops.
He yanks at its gills to reveal a mess of blood and bone
and flesh.　　　　All evening I have been tempted
by this neat metaphor: this staring at wave
and shadow, the feeding out of a net of language,
the need to disentangle each mesh to feed
out again after the shout goes up. Yes,
and the anchor, the boat etc – but the dead mullet
has put paid to that.　　　　What I need to know
is what the salmon know. How a shoal spawned
at the source of the Ray enters Ballyness Bay
and one leaps, knows they have come too far
　　　　so back they go –
away from this wrong source, the Tulloghobegly –
out the narrow neck of the bay, right into the Atlantic
and along the strand a mile or so till they reach the Ray.

What sensors, scents or pull of tide, what internal
geography, what physiology could navigate this?
I try to understand, learn, recall logic may only be
part of what goes on; today I sat with a friend, she
left with *I can hear that baby cry and must get
home* and I do not know how I will cope
with breasts full of milk that weep on hearing
a baby cry – still too scared I will be that girl again;
the simple lines of the self she knew altered
and she disowned a body she thought betrayed her
as a stranger's hands ground in its narrow neck,
swallowed a cry from a place so dark and deep
that it began to weep blood.
     I want to know what the salmon know.

Two Things Resound

Two things resound:
a friend's lover is a suicide,
another friend – her daughter sighs

with satisfaction, she is
on her way to study viola canina
and viola persicifolia. I quiz

her on violets and the specifics
of turloughs, these limestone lakes
that fill and dry with season, as if

it might obviate the white noise
of the other hows and whys;
how persicifolia survives submerged

to flower when the waters drain,
why canina cannot do the same;
how intent fingertips become

as the purpled-blues of petals
are compared and there must be,
running through all this,

there but for the grace of God ...
and perhaps that's why
these details release the scent

of a music as fragile
and unexpected
as a lake in bloom.

MEMORY IS THE TAIL

Memory, I think, is a substitute for the tail that
we lost for good in the happy process of evolution ...
                                                    – Joseph Brodsky

I want to clear a space in my mind
for the lambs I saw today –
three of them charging round the field
annoying the ewes, standing
with huge, quizzical ears,
their speckled brown and black markings
too big for them – then off again,
cantering at each other and the world,
tasting the roomy fields, so full of being just born.

I want more than the burnt-out volumes
I've been sifting since the fire.
The *Oxford English Dictionary*,
swollen by the heat, that makes me
want to cry – one of the few things
I'd rescued from the tranquil times.
Just visible is my father's name,
pencilled in in a careful hand,
my own under it in large, childish letters.

There is a black hole in my memory,
its gravity so dense it pulls me in some nights
so far I do not know if I will ever emerge.
I refuse to remember his drinking years.
Even later my stomach tightened when
he'd sniff a bottle of wine and sigh
or say, *a man could lose two days*
on poteen – all I know is that
you can lose a child there too.

ASPECTS OF PROMETHEUS

i

I squint at the brave February sun
and try to gauge how he stole fire.
Did he approach the Vulcan's forge
with a fennel bulb grasped tight,
eyes watering from a molten lava
that exhaled with gloop and hiss?
Or perhaps it was a splinter of more
solid fuel he took, like they once
did here from a visited hearth.
Here, routine still centres on fire
which I awkwardly follow, bending over
the squat range to rake the ashes
first thing each morning, bringing
out warm cinders which gust towards
Muckish. Later, as I watch hot coal
glimmer and shoot stars in the slack,
I recall that fire only became
mortal when he brought it back,
mortal like us, and must be tended.

ii

When I was a child the story
of this man haunted me –
I held a dark picture of Prometheus,
his back to the rocks, huge grey
waves that broke around him, chains
biting deeper as the beak of the
eagle approached. I did not know
why he was there.
What troubles me now, is Prometheus
after his release. Did he strain
each time a shadow crossed the sun,
though he was far from that rock?
Did tenderness, unwitting,
reopen the fragile wound
so he felt talons for each caress?
Perhaps he fingered his ring made
from shackle, not (as Zeus intended)
to evoke in him his torture but,
rather, to remind himself
that he was no longer there.

iii

But, what if it was a latter-day
Prometheus who stayed up
long hours to split the atom?
Awed by the wonder of its
component parts, was it he
who took uranium and pounded it,
pulling the protective skein apart?
And did they regret their catch, the
scientists who stole this fire
of the gods? Like Alfred Nobel
and dynamite? (Although more subtle
than an eagle and waves breaking
over rock, he carried the weight
of that, each night dreamt some
torment of the damned, to rise again
next day, made afresh).
The pilot of the *Enola Gay* says
that he felt no remorse, but in
Hiroshima their very shadows
were captured by the blast.

GINESTRA

Voices are raised in old Pompeii, a polyglot babble
as legions of tourists march through narrow streets
and spill over into the Forum. We stand surrounded
by columns that rise to balmy air. *Here candidates*
addressed the polis once, the guide shouts
over a clatter of kids racing past the grain mart.

The facts are; seventy-two loaves burnt that noon
in a bakery; eight thousand people fled Pompeii,
now daily this number returns; on Via d'Abundance
three women walk, raising dust on the stone footpath
slowly crossing from one side to the other.
Like jasmine the scent of a living town suffuses the air.

I suspect the two freed slaves, fortune made
in perfume, gaze down in delight (posterity assured)
as tours converge on their house, One Vicola dei Vetti,
and umbrella-wielding guides jockey for position
to lead us through the frescoed walls. A red
born of sulphur, mercury, bursts out into the room.

In the cool marble bath house (after *aahhs* at
stucco ceiling and mosaic floor) we stare into glass
cases at two who did not survive the stinking gas:
all flesh and bone decayed, a vacuum of themselves
encrusted in a hide of ash, their last contortions
caught in plaster and become maquette. They are too

vulnerable there, caught in mid-air. Do you think
they plead – not with a falling sky of ash, lapilli
and white-hot stone, but with us, who stare?
We'd already climbed Vesuvias that day – peered into

its gaping maw, at smoke that issued from nearby rocks
and the yellow torrent of *ginestra* that flows toward Naples.

THE COLOUR OF OIL

A man from Ogoniland
meets a fellow Nigerian
who knows nothing of oil,
laughs, *I don't know!*
Shrugs, *Green or yellow?*

I will tell you of oil,
replies the man from Ogoniland.
It is glutinous, he says,
It is ravenous, he says,
It is armed.

LEAC NA CUMHAÍ

I thought of you, Dad,
when I heard the story of Colmcille
and *leac na cumhaí*, the stone
that cures homesickness or loneliness.
The lovely ladies of Iona, you'd say,
of the time the piano was there,
with those two old women;
their large house in Dun Laoghaire
that had 'Iona' inscribed above the door.
That black piano was so much a part

of our lives, brought from London
back to Cork, and every perilous
move after. That, and the endless
lectures on: how the Irish would
not listen to classical music,
how Dublin was not the real Ireland
anyhow, only the Pale. Funny that,
after all, it was London you missed,
symbol of all you despised. (I found
it hard to keep up sometimes).

London, the terrain of your growing up,
and you had stories of close listening
to the radio for the late night broadcasts
from the Proms. Of getting cheap seats
at the Old Vic and seeing *all the greats,*
Gielguid, Olivier – eager to soak it all up.
Then, walking back to the small flat
on Sherland Road where my grandparents
lived close-knit lives with those
they knew from Cork, and the church –

all playing out a life of exile.
You'd been Cross Channel Dancing
champion at nine and Granny embroidered
intricate costumes for her blue-eyed son.
You told me once it was seagulls on
the Thames broke your heart, their
lonesome cadence so far from the sea.
That, if there was any animal you could be,
it would be a seagull, their clean white
shape so clear against the sky.

I think that was in Bray. Maybe walking
along the narrow path that wound around
the Head, where you'd christened all the spots:
the meander in the path from where
you could not see ahead or behind,
where the cliff sheered up on one side
and, on the other, below the crumbling wall,
fell in a dizzying drop to the sea;
the road to nowhere you called it,
I think, or was it *anywhere*?

Soon after you left for Mayo and sold
the piano. With the money bought a small,
green Ford – so you could get up to see
the three of us. (I had an image of you,
picking up unwary hitchhikers who you'd
interrogate about their politics; asking
why, oh why, did they not speak the Irish
language? It made the journey shorter,
you said). But as for the piano, I felt
its loss. It was as though you'd given up

on Mozart, Scott Joplin and Bach;
Johann Sebastian Bach, whose name
you pronounced with such care,

the 'fifth evangelist', and the only one
you'd kept faith with. Now instead, it was
Dessie's flute, the heavy wooden one
and you struggled with traditional tunes.
In Mayo you'd stand outside the house,
facing towards the bay, pitching a tune
to an echo that called and called back to you.

After your death, I found the small notebooks,
hard-backed, with the names of hundreds of tunes
written in your careful hand, neatly listed
and categorised, by date or name or something
else. A wish for order so counter-pointed
by the way you lived your life. With these sits
the *O'Neills* and the flute, carefully wrapped
in a old towel. Between them the large
D-whistle, your breath on aluminium
created its sweet rasp of a sound.

TRY AS I MIGHT

Try as I might I keep coming back to this,
circling loneliness until it settles here –
the fact, not of your death, but of prior loss.

The first time you left was when I was eight –
you went to dry out but nothing was said.
I was eleven the second time –
you moved down the road (nothing was said).
The third time was to live with 'her' –
we went to visit but nothing was said.

You had left a family before – two girls –
and when one turned up aged fourteen,
to meet her father, your response was,
It's too late for me but
it would be good for you three
to have a sister – you ring her.

For four whole years we lurched
through remissions with you.
Lymphoma emerged, receded, regrouped.

On the first anniversary of your death,
this time last year, the priest said that,
though it may feel like it now,
the history of the heart has not ended.

In making my peace with you
before you left this time
and more, in seeing you go,
in a one huge dawn breath
over the hills of Cork City,
the history of my heart has just begun.

CORK, FOR ME

Cork, for me is a litany:

hospice	radium	palliative
the Mercy	the Regional	the Union

and a bag of blood that falls,
drop by slow drop, into the vein.

The wrench of his sitting up
is like the sound of a whisper,
he's too weak to continue,
my father, in the corner bed of
the old Lord Mayor's place
which looks out to the marsh,
the sweep of the river
and the wrought iron bridge
where terns and seagulls settle.

REQUIEM
for my father

Walking once,
in the small council estate,
you marvelled at the telephone wires –
Look – a stave of endless potential,
miles of a clean score. And there were five lines
strung between each pole; each pole marked off a bar.

Perhaps, since music
is the silence between notes
and language the space between words,
perhaps, there are whole orchestras playing there
now.

PART III

TOPOGRAPHIES

o

My feet walk the lost topography
of a South London suburb;
through Burnt Ash Copse and St John's Wood
where tower blocks squat and lorries
kick up dust, down Verdant Hill to
Loampit Vale where buses whine to a halt.

o

Days when I am dumb, it is all I can do
to collect names, which, strung together
make a necklace of this city that might yet
ease the braced musculature of my throat:
Friendly Street and Stillness Lane
Silver Road and Nightingale Walk.

o

Beyond the Matalan and the MFI,
the Tesco and the KFC, between
the caff and the car park, runs Silk
Mills Path. Listen! Under the noise
of the traffic on the busy interchange
is the whirr of a loom, under the trundle
of the train is the clack of a shuttle;
and that dust in my mouth as I walk
under the junction, that dust is lint.

CAUGHT SAYING CHEESE FOR THE
PHOTOGRAPHER AT THE V&A

My puckered lips may give you a clue
as to how hard it is to sit and stare
at the glazed faces who pass me by –
they are boss-eyed from doing three
floors of oriental art (imagine).

I was stabled in the court of the Emperor
Han ... oh some three or four millennia ago
and there I lost my body to idiocy –
two noblemen lost in conflict over
The Book of Songs (of all things).

Oh, you should have heard the shattering
when they took the axe to me.
Look – below my neck is a deep scar
where it slipped and ate into jade flesh.
I had stood a full two hands before

but turned to see a pile of rubble
where once my flanks had been,
with only light to pick out
the scarred separation between neck
and bodiless space. Enough ...

in the last one thousand years
I have become accustomed
to living with just my head –
not happy you understand,
just accustomed.

MORE BEGUILING EVEN THAN THE BANKS OF DAFFS IN THE BOTANIC GARDENS, ARE THEIR NAMES

Spell binder   minnow   sun disc
Bell song   baby moon   acropolis

Cassata   pipit   Dutch master
Polar ice   petrel   rippling waters

Avalanche   apotheosa   old pheasant eye
Peeping Tom   Salomé   spell bound I.

GRANDMOTHER

The round table is cleared of
clutter, about your waist you
have knotted an apron, moist-
ened the brush with your tongue,

in front of you the full moon
of a porcelain plate; you hold
your breath – the wind stirs out
side, a goldfinch alights.

THE RIVER IS SWOLLEN

The river is swollen,
heavy-bellied,
heaving with city lights.

ISLAND SAYINGS

o

The scrapings of nine burnt pots
would put a dry cow back in milk.

o

Boil and drink the roots
of the yellow tormentil
to get shot of bunions.

o

At night we'd know the horses were back
from Gortahork – we'd hear their freshly
shod hooves sing out on the shingle.

o

The tide runs on old time here.

o

Tháinig na smaointe ar ais anseo,
as she dries dulse outside the door

o

I texted my son today, asked him
to bring milk from the mainland.

ERRIGAL

Translated from the Irish, *An tEargal*,
le Cathal Ó Searcaigh

Towards the end
your body stooped and hoary with age,
Errigal took possession of you.

Every once in a while you
were lifted clear of the earth
in its precipitous embrace.

Your eyes were alight,
imagination infused with its force,
its lour and lustre.

Heather sprouted on your sloping cheeks,
scraw on your eyes and lichen spread
from the crown of your head to your chin.

The long evening sun
soaked you in light, glittered in the quartz of your hair,
the granite of your forehead.

Your language became sharp and abrupt,
scree scudding down
the steep overhang of your tongue.

By degrees its doggedness,
the alchemy of its soil and allure of its sanctum
initiated you into the hereafter.

Now, when I look at the mountain,
you stare back at me from each crook and cleft.
You have taken possession of Errigal.

PERFORMANCE
for Donal O'Kelly and Trevor Knight

o

The two men leant in deep over the bridge,
hands on stone and elbows crooked for support
they peered farther in, mesmerised
by what they saw. 'It *is* a fish', said one.

o

'But I am a stone', said the fish,
'mottled and still in the sunlit water,
the taut muscle of my body as steady
as my neighbours who are sunk in silt,
around and over us the water flows.
Only my spine is so supple
that my tail wavers in the spate
and moves from its impression of rock.
Until then, movement is only light and shadow'.

o

'*I* am the fish', said the plastic bag,
snagged on a low rock in the river.
'Give me one fixed point
and the coursing water will flesh out
a body for me, mottle me with weed
and refracted light, so I become
fish that is stone
that is fish, till your eyes reach
frayed and streaming edges
which could not be tail –
this alone gives me away but till then,
substance is current and light'.

o

'God we're fools', the men laughed
as they walked away. 'City slickers
who can't even tell fish from stone
from rubbish in a stream'.

o

Back under the bridge and the river coursed on,
stone became fish turned to plastic
and spoke,
'I think they put on a play last night.
I heard that in the dark, gas heater-hum
of an old church hall, the audience peered
up at that man who became gull and,
as his shoulders rose,
his elbows led the wing-tips of his wrists
to hover over seas and in the sky of the stage.

He was squawk and flap, wave-slop wing-flip
till he alit when, with the pivot of a foot
and a single gesture that possessed him,
became in turn:
sailor, lover, father, mother,
convict, crew and governor,
most beautiful of all though
he was child to the father
as her voice rang out
from the altered muscles of his throat
papa's home'.

o

'Aye', said the stone.

o

'And *I* heard', said plastic to fish,
'how the other sat deep in a pool of blue light,
and his fingers sent storm
and rain, horse-hoof and oar-creak
to reverberate through the hall
and each body there,
that in the moment the whale let out
a discarnate scream
it crackled up each spine
so they smelt salt and fear and dying whale.
They filed out silent, bemused at finding earth
when their feet thought they'd meet
the deep roll of the ocean'.

PICTURE
for Una Campbell

A glimmer of white butterflies,
fed on your cabbages, rises among the reeds,
hovers round the splay of each stalk.
They flaunt the green scribble of gorse; set off
the foothills of Errigal; rise to its broad strokes
of silver and grey sweep of scree which swoops
to the gouge left by a glacier, whose only constants
are shifting cloud and light.
                                 Errigal always sets up
this puzzle of what is symbol and what just is,
and that which compels us to make marks. Was
it you told me of Mount Fuji? How those
in its shadow won't eye it direct but watch
its picture on the wall – awe,
but keeps its moods at bay too.
                                      I stare through
this wall of glass you have built in Sroughan,
and I think you would laugh at this story I heard:
a travelling photographer at a farmer's door,
tries to sell him an image of his land, *And why*
would I spend fifty quid on that, says he,
when I can step out myself and see
the bucking thing for free?
                           Still,
I retreat to the solid walls of your back room
to make this picture where a glimmer of white
butterflies, fed on your cabbages, rises.

GLASS

Shelved in the potent scent of musty books
and dusty floors sits the full *Encyclopaedia
Britannica.* A child and her father look
for glass, finding it in Volume IV
between 'fulgurite' and 'hyalopsite';
in her project book she draws
glass beads and a Phoenician kneeling at a fire
and loves the sound of Pliny who told of this and more.

She collects worn glass down at the shore,
hand and eye hover and flash among pebbles.
The unceasing tide a lapidary of broken bottles
but in reverse – muting clear to milky white,
the gleam of brown become opaque,
their stinging edges softened and light.

Rudolph Blaschka

nineteenth-century glass-maker of marine
animals and the Harvard Botanical Collection

I was born the year of the first orchids,
and fancy that, as my fingers stretched
in their amniotic fluid, my father's hands
were gesturing spun glass to stamen.

As I lay in my cradle the rhythm
of the treadle steadied me, once on ground
nothing would do me but to fetch
tongs and rods of glass until bidden

to bed. Still in my teens when the marine
collection began, I obsessed about
the exact opalescence of the squid,
sought the cerulean of the sea slug

until, drop by drop, was immersed
in the creation of a single-celled plankton.

BREATH

Verses from the Qur 'an encircle us – an intense
calligraphy glazed onto walls dense
with cedar carving and white plaster, in the centre
a fountain which stipples the air with water.

It is forbidden, the guide tells us, to paint the likeness
of the human form or carve it from stone *unless*
you can breathe life into it and who but God ...
But listen! The heat is punctuated by the call to prayer,

it rises, plangent through the air,
reverberating in the base of the throat, welling up all *ul-*
ul lah, uh-lah; each vowel created deep within the lung,
consonants by the muscle of the tongue

and hinge of jaw so breath has sung
word (or word breath) and what is scripted becomes.

IRAQI SEED BANK, 2000

In an airless room in Abu Ghraib
my colleagues and I begin to sift
for seven strains of wheat, and know,
without words, that the first must
be from Jarmo near Kirkuk; we pick

the modest seed of einkorn, sown
eight thousand years and more,
so each thresh and winnow sing
of the birth of cultivation and place
it in a pocket of the black box. Next

wild liquorice and tamarind
that flourish by the Tigris,
linseed from Irbil,
sesame from Mosul,
millet from Tikrit,

six-row barley, with a language
as dense as a Sumarian script
and all the unread literature
of the cuniform, two row barley
of the people of Babylonia

and on and on until this box, bound
for Syria, is full. In an airless room
in Abu Ghraib, I name each seed
one thousand times so each in turn
shall bear one thousand more.

Nell Regan was born in London in 1969 and grew up in Dublin. A graduate of University College, Dublin and The Poets' House, Donegal/Lancaster University, she has worked as a researcher and currently teaches in Dublin. Her poetry has been widely published and anthologised, and was awarded third place in the 2006 Patrick Kavanagh Awards. She has also published several critical pieces including biographical research on Helena Molony in *Female Activists, Irish Women and Change, 1900-1960* and in *The Field Day Anthology*, Vol 4. *Preparing for Spring* is her debut collection.